WHY DO ASTRONAUTS WEAR SPACESUITS?

 Gareth Stevens
Publishing

BY MICHAEL PORTMAN

Please visit our website, www.garethstevens.com. For a free color catalog of all our high-quality books, call toll free 1-800-542-2595 or fax 1-877-542-2596.

Library of Congress Cataloging-in-Publication Data

Portman, Michael.
Why do astronauts wear spacesuits? / by Michael Portman.
  p.cm. — (Space mysteries)
Includes index.
ISBN 978-1-4339-9239-1 (pbk.)
ISBN 978-1-4339-9240-7 (6-pack)
ISBN 978-1-4339-9238-4 (library binding)
1. Astronauts—Juvenile literature. 2. Astronautics—Juvenile literature. I. Portman, Michael, 1976- II. Title.
TL793.P67 2014
629.45—dc23

First Edition

Published in 2014 by
Gareth Stevens Publishing
111 East 14th Street, Suite 349
New York, NY 10003

Designer: Katelyn E. Reynolds
Editor: Therese Shea

Photo credits: Cover, p. 1 Photo by SSPL/Getty Images; cover, pp. 1, 3–32 (background texture) David M. Schrader/Shutterstock.com; pp. 3–32 (fun fact graphic) © iStockphoto.com/spxChrome; pp. 5, 11, 15, 19, 25, 26, 27 NASA; p. 7 NASA Earth Observatory/Wikipedia.com; p. 9 NASA/Wikipedia.com; p. 10 NASA/Regan Geeseman; pp. 13, 17 NASA/AFP/Getty Images; p. 21 Don Emmert/AFP/Getty Images; p. 23 NASA via Getty Images; p. 29 Stocktrek Images/Getty Images.

Printed in the United States of America

CPSIA compliance information: Batch #CS13GS: For further information contact Gareth Stevens, New York, New York at 1-800-542-2595.

CONTENTS

Dreaming of Space 4

Comfortable Earth 6

It's Dusty Up There 8

The First Spacesuits 10

Mercury Spacesuits.. 12

Gemini Spacesuits 14

Apollo Spacesuits 16

Hot or Cold 18

Space Shuttle 20

The ISS 22

The EMU 24

Puzzle Pieces.. 26

Suiting Up for Mars.. 28

Glossary.. 30

For More Information 31

Index.. 32

Words in the glossary appear in **bold** type the first time they are used in the text.

DREAMING OF SPACE

For centuries, people have dreamed of traveling in space. Building a spacecraft to do that was the first **challenge**. But figuring out a way for people to move around in space outside the craft was an even bigger challenge.

There's no oxygen to breathe in space. In Earth's **orbit**, temperatures can be as cold as –250°F (–157°C) and as high as 250°F (121°C). Fortunately, spacesuits are made to protect astronauts from these and other dangers.

5

COMFORTABLE EARTH

A thick layer of gases called the atmosphere surrounds Earth. The atmosphere is what allows us to breathe. It's what keeps Earth from getting too hot or too cold. Earth's atmosphere also protects us from most of the sun's harmful rays.

Since there's no atmosphere in space, people couldn't breathe there. In fact, it would take only about 15 seconds for someone in space to fall **unconscious**. They'd also be exposed to harmful solar **radiation** and extreme temperatures.

OUT OF THIS WORLD!
An astronaut's blood could boil and freeze in space.

Earth's atmosphere shields us from a variety of dangers found in space.

7

IT'S DUSTY UP THERE

Space is full of tiny dust particles called micrometeorites. Micrometeorites fly through space at very high speeds. Even something as small as a grain of sand can cause great harm if it's traveling fast enough.

A spacesuit must protect an astronaut from micrometeorites. It must also provide oxygen and a **pressurized** atmosphere. A spacesuit should keep the body in a comfortable temperature at all times. In addition, it needs to allow an astronaut to move around easily.

OUT OF THIS WORLD!

An astronaut in a spacesuit needs to have a way to talk with other astronauts as well as people on Earth.

Besides many other needs, astronauts must be able to see out of their helmets!

9

THE FIRST SPACESUITS

Early spacesuits were based on pressurized flight suits worn by jet pilots. Jet aircraft sometimes fly so high that there's not enough oxygen or air pressure for people to function.

Jet flight suits were made of rubber-coated **material** that would blow up, or inflate, like a balloon if air pressure became too low. The inflatable layer was worn inside another layer that kept the suit from expanding too much. Hoses attached to the suit provided oxygen to the pilot.

modern jet flight suit

OTHER RESCUE SIDE

LITTLE JOE

X-1E

Pressurized flight suits were only meant to work if a jet lost cabin pressure.

MERCURY SPACESUITS

The Mercury program was the first US manned-spaceflight program. Mercury astronauts wore spacesuits that were based on the pressurized suits worn by navy pilots. The outer part of the Mercury suits was made of several layers of **aluminum**-coated material.

Mercury astronauts never exited their spacecraft in space. Their suits were **designed** only to be worn inside the spacecraft. The Mercury spacesuits only had to provide pressure and oxygen if the craft had an **emergency**.

OUT OF THIS WORLD!
From 1961 to 1963, the Mercury program completed six manned spaceflights.

The Mercury spacesuits were cooled by air with a fan connected to the suit.

13

GEMINI SPACESUITS

Gemini was the second American spaceflight program and the first time astronauts took spacewalks. The Gemini spacesuits had to remain connected to the spacecraft during spacewalks. This is because they didn't have a built-in life-support system.

The Gemini suits had layers of a material called Teflon that protected the astronauts from micrometeorites. The suits weren't very comfortable, and they didn't cool the astronauts well. Sweat made their helmets fog up. Scientists looked for ways to improve the suits.

OUT OF THIS WORLD!

From 1965 to 1966, the Gemini program flew 10 manned spaceflights.

14

The cord attaching the astronauts to the spacecraft was called the umbilical cord.

15

APOLLO SPACESUITS

The spacesuits used in the Apollo program were designed for a new purpose. The Apollo missions aimed to put astronauts on the moon for the first time.

Walking on the moon is very different from floating in space. The Apollo spacesuits had to protect astronauts while they were on the rocky surface of the moon. The suits had their own life-support systems that allowed astronauts to explore the moon without being connected to the landing craft.

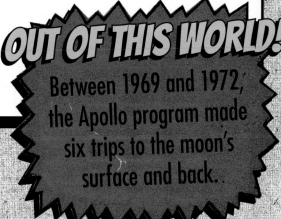

OUT OF THIS WORLD!

Between 1969 and 1972, the Apollo program made six trips to the moon's surface and back.

19

HOT OR COLD

The Apollo spacesuits kept the astronauts comfortable in extreme cold or heat, as well as protected them from micrometeorites and jagged rocks on the surface of the moon. The Apollo suits were cooled with water instead of air. This made the spacesuits much more comfortable than the Gemini spacesuits.

To protect the astronauts' eyes from harsh sunlight, special **visors** were built into the helmets. These visors could be raised or lowered by the astronauts.

OUT OF THIS WORLD!

The Apollo spacesuits weighed 180 pounds (82 kg) on Earth, but only 30 pounds (14 kg) on the moon.

The Apollo Lunar Extravehicular Visor Assembly (LEVA) protected the astronauts from sunlight. The visor was coated with gold.

19

SPACE SHUTTLE

After the Apollo missions ended, astronauts stopped traveling to the moon. Instead, they used the space shuttle to orbit Earth. Shuttle missions included maintaining the Hubble Space Telescope and bringing supplies to the International Space Station.

During takeoffs and landings, space shuttle astronauts wore orange spacesuits similar to those worn by the Apollo astronauts. These suits were designed to pressurize only in emergencies, if the pressure in the cabin of the spacecraft failed. Later spacesuits also contained a **parachute** and an inflatable life preserver.

OUT OF THIS WORLD!

The space shuttle program lasted from 1981 until 2011 and included 135 manned spaceflights.

Space shuttle *Atlantis* astronauts wave before boarding the spacecraft in 2011.

21

THE ISS

The International Space Station (ISS) is the largest man-made structure in space. The ISS is a floating **laboratory** used by many countries. Astronauts working outside the ISS wear spacesuits called Extravehicular Mobility Units (EMUs). EMUs are basically minispacecraft. Each costs about $12 million!

In the past, spacesuits were specially designed for each astronaut. EMUs are made of separate pieces, and their parts can be mixed and matched to fit astronauts of different sizes.

OUT OF THIS WORLD!

The ISS can be seen from Earth without a telescope if you know when and where to look.

Astronauts working in a spacesuit for several hours need water. The EMU has an In-suit Drink Bag!

23

THE EMU

The EMU is made of several pieces that fit together. Some parts are soft and bendable, while others are made of hard material. The soft sections are made up of 13 separate layers.

One of the most important pieces of an EMU is called the Hard Upper Torso (HUT). The HUT is made of **fiberglass** and covers an astronaut's chest. The arms, legs, helmet, backpack, and life-support system all connect to the HUT.

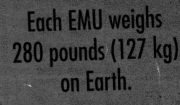

OUT OF THIS WORLD!
Each EMU weighs 280 pounds (127 kg) on Earth.

Small jets on the backpack of an EMU allow an astronaut to fly back to the space station if they float too far away.

25

Much like the Apollo spacesuits, today's EMUs use water to keep astronauts cool. Before putting on the outer EMU, an astronaut first gets into the Liquid Cooling and Ventilation Garment (LCVG). The LCVG is a piece of clothing with tubes woven into it. Water is pumped through the tubes. The LCVG covers everything but an astronaut's head, hands, and feet.

Putting on a spacesuit is no easy task. There's a 25-step process to prepare for a spacewalk!

preparing for a spacewalk

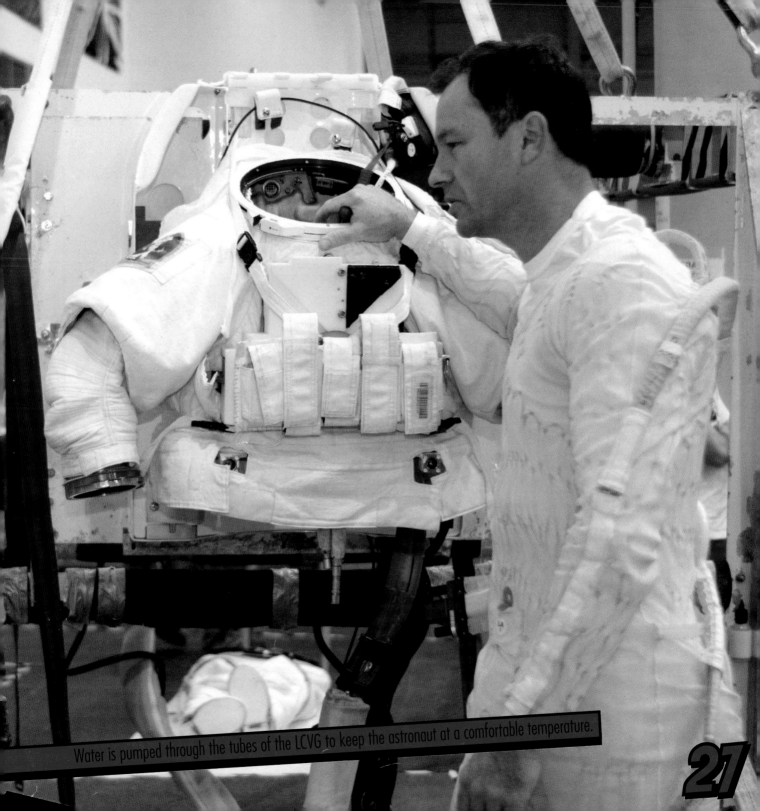

Water is pumped through the tubes of the LCVG to keep the astronaut at a comfortable temperature.

27

SUITING UP FOR MARS

In the future, NASA (National Aeronautics and Space Administration) hopes to send astronauts to the surface of Mars. Exploring Mars will be very challenging. It has more **gravity** than the moon. Current spacesuits would be too heavy to wear on Mars. An astronaut wouldn't be able to move!

Unlike the moon, Mars is very windy. Dust storms on Mars could severely harm a spacesuit. NASA is designing new spacesuits that are stronger, lighter, and more protective than what astronauts wear now.

SPACESUIT FIRSTS

A Russian astronaut, Alexey Leonov, took the first spacewalk on March 18, 1965.

Edward White II was the first NASA astronaut to take a spacewalk on June 3, 1965.

On July 20, 1969, Neil Armstrong became the first man to walk on the moon.

Alan Shepard hit golf balls on the moon on February 6, 1971. They're still there!

On October 11, 1984, Katherine Sullivan became the first American woman to walk in space.

The longest spacewalk took place on March 11, 2001. It lasted for 8 hours and 56 minutes.

NASA tested new spacesuits in Antarctica's freezing, windy conditions.

GLOSSARY

aluminum: a type of lightweight metal

challenge: a test of abilities

design: to create the pattern or shape of something

emergency: an unexpected situation that needs quick action

fiberglass: glass fibers pressed into a hard material. Used in making various products.

gravity: the force that pulls objects toward the center of a planet, moon, or star

laboratory: a place with tools to perform experiments

material: something used to make something, such as a fabric

orbit: to travel in a circle or oval around something, or the path used to make that trip

parachute: a specially shaped piece of cloth that collects air to slow something down

pressurize: to maintain a normal air pressure in a space

radiation: waves of energy

unconscious: unable to see, hear, or sense what is happening because of accident or injury

visor: a front part of a helmet, made of see-through material, and used to protect the face or eyes

FOR MORE INFORMATION

BOOKS

Dyer, Alan. *Space*. New York, NY: Simon & Schuster Books for Young Readers, 2007.

Stott, Carole. *Space Exploration*. New York, NY: Dorling Kindersley, 2010.

Young, Amanda. *Spacesuits Within the Collections of the Smithsonian National Air and Space Museum*. Brooklyn, NY: PowerHouse Books, 2009.

WEBSITES

The History of Spacesuits
www.nasa.gov/audience/forstudents/k-4/stories/history-of-spacesuits-k4.html
See photos of spacesuits and read how they've changed over the years.

How Space Suits Work
science.howstuffworks.com/space-suit4.htm
Use an interactive diagram to locate different parts of the EMU.

What Is a Spacesuit?
www.nasa.gov/audience/forstudents/5-8/features/what-is-a-spacesuit-58.html
Read NASA's description of the spacesuits astronauts depend on to keep them alive.

INDEX

air pressure 10, 11, 12, 20
aluminum 12
Apollo program 16, 18, 19, 20, 26
atmosphere 6, 7, 8
backpack 24, 25
emergency 12, 20
Extravehicular Mobility Units (EMUs) 22, 23, 24, 25, 26
fiberglass 24
flight suits 10, 11, 12
Gemini program 14, 18
Hard Upper Torso (HUT) 24
helmets 9, 14, 18, 24
Hubble Space Telescope 20

inflatable life preserver 20
International Space Station 20, 22, 25
life-support system 14, 16, 24
Liquid Cooling and Ventilation Garment (LCVG) 26, 27
Lunar Extravehicular Visor Assembly 19
Mars 28
Mercury program 12, 13
micrometeorites 8, 14, 18
moon 16, 17, 18, 20, 28, 29

NASA 28, 29
oxygen 4, 8, 10, 12
parachute 20
pressurized 8, 10, 11, 12, 20
radiation 6
spacecraft 4, 12, 14, 15, 20, 21
space shuttle 20, 21
spacewalks 14, 26, 29
Teflon 14
temperature 4, 6, 8, 27
umbilical cord 15
visors 18, 19